AFFRILACHIA

poems by

FRANK X WALKER

OLD COVE PRESS

LEXINGTON, KENTUCKY 2000

Published by
OLD COVE PRESS
oldcove.com

Composed in Bembo
Prepress services by Beau Graphics, Lexington
Printed and bound by Thomson-Shore, Inc., Dexter, MI
Printed on 60# Natures Book Natural

Acknowledgments
For important assistance in making this book:
Aaron Anderson, Sharon Bailey, Teresa Burgett,
Jean Donohue, Jonathan Greene, Myra Hughes,
Fred Johnson, Larry Treadway, Minh Truong,
Duncan Veach, and Mike Zender.

ISBN 0-9675424-0-5

Printed in the U.S.A.

Publisher's Cataloging-in-Publication Data
Walker, Frank X
Affrilachia / poems by Frank X Walker.
Lexington, KY: Old Cove Press, 2000.
p. cm.
ISBN 0-9675424-0-5
1. Afro-Americans – Kentucky – Poetry. I. Title

FIRST EDITION
Ninth Printing

AFFRILACHIA

for Faith A. Smith and Frank Walker, Sr.

Contents

Affrilachia

Clifton I

We stood there
me, him, regret
crowding the edge of the road
same nose
same hands
same nervous smile
casualties
in a civil rights era
divorce war

stood in the mud
in the sane
pretending to be father and son
shadow and tree
finger and thumb
again
avoiding each other's eyes
biting bottom lips
hoping we left our pain
in the city

staring at the edge of his unlit cigarette
I search for answers
I wait for clarity
and or flames

hidden among the lessons
in the stories
he pulls from his pockets
like peppermint candy
covered with lint

we wander through
the family resting place
at the rear of the church
on a crooked hill
just beyond the old outhouse, a two-seater
searching for his grandmother's
marker
among the Trumbos
Terrances
Rowes
and rows of soldiers

nodding at a gravel road
made more visible
through naked winter trees
and a spot opposite
the old schoolhouse
at the edge of the cliff
he said
'papa george's daddy died
right about there'
said
'a runaway team a horses

missed the turn
and plunged over the cliff'
said
'his head musta hit a tree
on the way down'

peering out over the water
he mused about
a giant black dolphin of a man
who used to swim up and down the river
on his back
face up like a log
said he could swim that good

he took me to his favorite spot
to where he played as a boy
where clark's run
empties into herrington lake
in a ceremonious succession
of slate and limestone steps
that both walked and crawled
the descending one hundred yards
free falling like a Caribbean mountain
waterfall
ten feet at a time
before splashes
softened into ripples
then drowned

we walked the land
then stood there
in the mud
crowding the road
again
family history clinging
to our souls
his stories
floating in the air
like vapor photographs

we stood
at the edge of the road
in Clifton
looking out at the
wide wet mirror
that divided
one county from the next
absence from forgiveness
then spoke and laughed
in unison
like twins
like a small choir
singing psalms

Wishbone

often times
parents
at that fork in the road
grab on to their end
like the smallest part of the wishbone
close their eyes
and snap
and wish
nothing but pain and suffering
and revenge
on their now-severed halves
the used to be
'til death do us part kiss me lips
now scream
kiss my ass
and you can raise those snotty-nosed kids
by yourself

iron will
and skillets
answered with such venom
that he left believing
only a crazy man would have stayed
though he never saw
the butcher's knife

that was stopped in its path
by the back door he slammed
for the last time

he never looked back
at the puddle of woman
he had snatched
from a high-school honors program
and awarded apron strings
traded her diploma for
two thousand one hundred and ninety days
in a role of diaper duty
instead
he sprouted wings
and carried all of his paycheck
to another nest
took off his shoes
in a prettier place
with nicer things
a place unlittered with crumb snatchers
and pretended
he never
gave his name away
never said
'i do'
never looked back

thirty years later
he stands much shorter
than his photograph

and moves without the same decisiveness
that used to carry him out
of the same stores
or into a back room
if we were sent to visit
on his payday
granny always said
he'd come crawling back
mamma said
she couldn't wait that long
and gave her love
and four more kids
to men
who made her feel young
again

often times
parents
mamas and papas
at that fork in the road
grab on to their end
like the smallest part
of the wishbone
close their eyes
…and
snap

Statues of Liberty

mamma scrubbed
rich white porcelain
and hard wood floors
on her hands and knees
hid her pretty face and body
in sack dresses
and aunt jemima scarves
from predators
who assumed
for a few extra dollars
before christmas
in dark kitchen pantries
they could unwrap her
present

aunt helen, her sister
took in miss emereen's laundry
every Saturday morning
sent it back
hand washed, air dried,
starched
ironed, folded
and cleaner
than any professional service

she waited patiently
for her good white woman
to die
and make good on her promise
to leave her
a little something
only to leave her first

aunt bertha, the eldest
exported her maternal skills
to suburbia
to provide surrogate attention
to children of money and privilege
and spent every other moment
preaching about
the richness of the afterlife
before the undertaker
took her
to see for herself

housekeepers
washer women
maids
a whole generation
of portable day care centers
traded their days for dimes

allowing other women
the freedom to shop
and sunbathe
the opportunity to school
or work

this curse-swallowing sorority
dodged dicks
and bosses
before postwar women
punched clocks
they birthed civil and human rights
gave the women's movement
legs
sacrificed their then
to pave the way for a NOW
their hard-earned pennies
sent us off to college
and into the world
our success is their reward
we
are their monuments
but they
are our statues of liberty

Matriarch

mother margaret
raised hell
held her liquor
hated referees
and white rules
and measured every man
by her vision of
joe louis
said king was
sick in the head
for not fighting back
and that jesse
would never amount
to much of anything
she got an attitude
when the mail was late
bit into the butt
of every excuse
with a
'well, why not fool?'
and never
apologized
to anyone
not even at the end
when she snubbed her nose
at science

went home and lived
well beyond
the twenty-three hours
the doctors
gave her
she used to warn
that a snapping turtle
wouldn't let loose
until lightning struck
but this great grand matron
was overqualified
to wear that shell
because she would never
bury her young in the sand
and leave them
unprotected

likened to porcupines
and other beasts of pray
mother margaret
was no parishioner
and she raised
black panthers

Cease Fire

there were no mirrors
at our house
browns stared into greens
kinky pondered straight
burnt brass fingers fondled
locks of gold

they say people
fall in love
with their own reflections
that daughters
look for someone
like their fathers
but my yoruba-faced sisters
all married white boys
my brothers and nephews
do not discriminate
collecting ebony and ivory
prom pictures
like trophies
believing all of the words
to the preamble
consecrating their mtv choices
with white chocolate babies
with hair
their mothers
can't comb

birthing human treaties
in a domestic race war
and I am caught in the middle
at the peace conference
bullet holes in my memories
bayonet around my neck
negotiating cease fires
with families
whose maiden names
are
enemy

Rock Star

my sistah loves rocks
she'll do anything
for a piece of
hard candy
my sistahz
a rock star
passed her on the street
she didn't even see me
through her tinted windows
my sistahz a mountain
when I call up to her
my 'I love you's'
get lost
in the valleys
my sister's on crack
we only see her
between highs and buys
she be all nervous
and shit
rubbing the back of her hand
like it's some kinda
magic lamp
so we all
stand around and wish
all the dope
in the world
would turn into penny candy

'cause my sister got a sweet tooth
an' mamma swears
she'll pull it out
before she give her up
to sugar

Crooked Afro

daddy don't smile
when you ask 'bout
uncle jay
my favorite
drunk or sober

unk got bookoo years
fo shootin'
a man
inna club

this man's man
had already done time
in 'nam
wasn't back but a minute
when this otha
tour of duty
called

a stretch in eddyville
would be nuthin'
but a slow dance
he said

but when he tripped home
one easter
to his fatha's funeral
and stood at the coffin in cuffs
the music stopped

when we welcomed him back
he came to the party
without his dancing shoes
his record skipping
singing a song
that old lovers
and ex-teammates
had already put in the attic

now half of him
and a crooked afro
roam the streets
and alleys
borrowing just enough
for another bottle
to make love to

hoping to find somebody
who still listens
to isaac hayes or
little stevie wonder
on eight tracks

and remembers when
he could just take over a game
if the bate bulldogs
were behind
and the cheerleaders
called his name

daddy don't smile
when you ask 'bout uncle jay
and some of us
still cry
when he tries
to dance

Hummingbird

midnight
and somebody I know
is dead
from AIDS
at thirty-seven
they're not even flying
him home
gonna plant him in Cali
give away all his shit
and come back to Kentucky
believing nobody ever knew
the truth
family never talked about
him being gay
and didn't defend him
when others called him
punk, faggot or sissy
just believed he was different
flighty maybe
a little girlish
but really really really
sweet
too sweet for the navy

his daddy's heavy hand
never touched his
pretty face
and his eyelashes turned
to hummingbirds
waiting for his mother
to love him back
it's midnight
now somebody you know
is dead
from AIDS
at thirty-seven

Death by Basketball

Before and after school
he stood
on a milk crate
eyeballed the mirror
and only saw wayne turner
at tournament time

a third grader
just off the bus
barely four feet
off the ground
he dropped his books
sank a j'
from the top of the key
and heard the crowd roar
beat his man off the dribble
with a break yaneck
crossover
and slammed himself
on the cover of a box
of wheaties

he was out there
every night
under a street light

fighting through double picks
talking trash
to imaginary body checks
'you can't hold me fool'
fake right
'this is my planet'
drive left
'is the camera on'
reverse lay-up
'that's butter baby'
finishing with a trey
from downtown, swish!
'I'm inna zone t'night
whogotnext?'
more than a little
light in the ass
hands so small
the ball almost dribbled him
he formed his own lay-up line
in the bluegrass
wildcat jersey
hanging like a summer dress
on a court made bald
from daily use
and instead of writing
his spelling words
he signed a contract
he could barely read

inked a commitment
in big block letters
to the NBA
and NIKE
and SPRITE
scribbled superstar in cursive
with a fat red pencil
and practiced his
million dollar smile
not his multiplication table
thinking of how many
chocolate milks
he could buy
with his signing bonus
or his all-star game
appearance fee
after recess

another shooting
another tragic death
another little genius
who will never test out
of a dream
that kills legitimate futures
every night
under street lights
wherever these products
are sold

Neapolitan

my niggaz
my niggaz
my microwave niggaz
you neo-hoodlum
hip hop intellectuals
changing flavors
and directions
like a kennedy bullet
why you'll be brand new
before I finish this poem
eluding the fashion police
turning hair salons
into art museums
making old new
always the prototype
never xerox
taking muzak
way past the fifth dimension
accompanied by movements
that eclipse jazz
supercede the most complicated danze
challenging
universal laws
quantifying spontaneity
changing matter

bending light
illustrating perpetual motion
and thought
and action
damn!
reinvent the will
and you'll be jockin'
solar-powered
stained glass pyramids

oh, that was last week
I'm buggin'

CP Time

we be rapping
about time
about
being on it
and in it
this colored people's clock thang
an appendage
more like
fried chicken
and watermelon
and less like inventing jazz
or building pyramids
this black fingerprint
that dis-colors us
based on western standards
designed to ignore
cultural differences
that say
it/we
are cyclical by design
and not linear
is now on trial

when it is understood
that it is natural
to resist oppression
we will change
that CP to
communal potential time
because our innate rhythm
our internal clocks
dictate that to be
in truth
in sync
with the universe
we must do it
whatever our it is
when
and only when
it feels right
and not because assimilation
rang the bell

to do otherwise
is to surrender
a now-impossible task
since
marcus garvey painted all our
white flags
red black and green

so let it be known
that the original
hue men (and women)
even in our present
captive states
(kentucky not excluded)
still be chiming
to the cyclical rhythm
of the universe
so don't confuse our tardiness
with laziness or irresponsibility
we who are rebels
by western standards
will be
who we are
all the time
and when
our life cycles
end
and ancestral ones begin
may the timekeeper note that
though we may have always been late
we were always
right on
time

Lil' Kings

what if
the good revren doctah
mlk jr
was just marty
or lil' king
not a pastor
but a little faster
from the streets
quoting gangsta rap
not gandhi

was not dr. king
but king doctah
or ice-k
his peace sign on a gold tooth
or gleaming 14 karat like
from around his neck

what if somebody
screaming 'nigger'
hit 'im in the head
with a brick
and he pulled out a nine
and squeezed off
one or two rounds
not tears

praying
only that he
not miss
sported mlk
on phat brass knuckles
and a left-handed
diamond pinky ring
walked the streets
with his home boyz
spray painting
let freedom ring
and I had a dream
on bus stops
and stop signs

got arrested for
conspiring to incite riots
disturbing the peace
and resisting arrest

didn't preach from
no pulpit
but on a microphone
behind turntables
mixin' and scratchin'
listenin' to dr. dre
wu tang
and the notorious b.i.g.

pants down to his hightops
hat on backwards
eyes on a prized new voice
not no bel
no peace
of nothin'
that just rings
when it's hit
a voice that
hits back

could he still
be king?

Sweet B
(for Betty Shabazz)

this close to death
to malcolm
why would she choose
to live?

a miniature malcolm
carrying the weight
of his grandfather's name
poured out an accelerant
an anti-libation
around a woman
who has been burned
been bombed
been banned
by family
before

why would she choose
to stay
with those
who pilgrimage daily
to shrines
of nonviolence
in a city
full of everything but

with those who
know not where her
warrior husband's body
rests
in anonymity
she couldn't just
die
how could she
malcolm never did

simply another transition
spokesdaughter attilah said
not death
and now
she doesn't have to choose
between shepherding for six
or sharing
a constellation
with her
X

Violins or Violen...ce

empty
depleted
dust dry tears
not drops
like tumbleweeds
rolling down
across my face
aching still for the children
hands cracked
from giving
fatigued
from filling sandbags
and sand hearts
with all that we are
trying to counter
not erase
years of neglect
generations of not knowing
not believing the difference
between
violins
and violen...ce

face to face
with certified
menaces to society

used to be
boyz in the hood
who come to us
in stereo
music jacked up so loud
the bass
jump-starts their hearts
every time they die
in their sleep
who bounce into the room
pants hip hopped
down low
rapped around imaginary waist
where their manseed
not manhood
should be
malnourished
from love deficient
hug-less diets
gangster rap lyrics
movies
and statistics
that scream
IF YOU SEE A BLACK FACE
IN THE MIRROR

KILL IT!
and that beautiful sistah
is just somebody's ho or bitch
and YO MAMMA...

you cannot defuse
legitimate anger
with a government check
from behind a desk
or by passing a collection plate
what is faith to those
who measure their lives
not with calendars
but with stopwatches
noosed comfortably
around their necks
who stay up all night
and live every minute
like it's too short
or the last
one

with faded twisted
bald dreaded heads
that are simply
bus stops
for eyes
that haven't closed
since way before

x, rodney and king
even before tuskegee experiments
lynchings
and castrations

eyes that don't remember shut
that refuse to even blink
'less they miss some vital part
of their choreographed
insignificance

how do you fill up
the sometimes empty vessels
they are
as 911
becomes their reality
while old age
and equal opportunity
is just smoke
from a gun
fired point blank
at the symptom
and not the disease

these children
claim their manhood early
because they might not be here
when it comes

they raise hell
'cause nobody raised them

they worship defiant outspoken
light and sound shows

armed with remote controls
they select entertainment
over education
as if they're on death row
and are requesting
one last feel good
before they go out
with a bang
and they will
because they never heard
of medgar evers
a family man
and activist
shot in the back
in his own driveway
never heard of
fred hampton
betrayed by another panther
killed in his sleep
by the fbi
never heard of stephen biko
a freedom fighter
beaten to death
by authorities
in a holding cell
never heard of huey newton
or his breakfast program
never heard a grown man cry
never heard of you
or i

we can say it's
not our problem
or we can be solutions
we can blame it all
on the man
or we can be solutions
we can just give up
and burn it all down
we can let these children
our children
all children
drown in their own blood
or we can be
solutions

if this nightmare was just a fairy tale
it would be real easy
to feel like the ugly frog
and wait for a beautiful princess
to come along and kiss us
but don't it make more sense
to just kiss yourself
and hop the hell
on into history
and
be solutions

Taking the Stares

I remember
stomping around campus
in black boots and fatigues
nappy head and brain
tongue of fire
my visible politics
making me a human hand grenade

now I stare down at shined black Bostonians
or soft calfskin Cole Haans
designer silk ties
and the French cuffs
on my lightly starched white shirt
on an elevator ride
to a private office
with a picturesque view
of the city
still amazed
at perks
like cell phones
company credit cards
ford explorers and laptop computers

the enemy would never
see me coming

then a brother I pass on the street
yells
'sold out Uncle Tom ass nigga'
at me
with a sneer
with his eyes
as he recognizes
his distaste for my image
and spits it out on the concrete
towards a bottomless
metal grate

as it hangs there
I suddenly remember
seventeen years
in the projects
free lunch
commodities
welfare checks
food stamps
working three part-time
service jobs
to feed my kids
walking everywhere
trying to remain tall
even though my money
was short

today
my office is on the top floor
but I avoid the elevator
that welcome pain in my calves
and the fire in my lungs
has become the bass line
and the melody
for the jazz prayer
I speak between the stares
I am praying for strength
for strength to always be black and blessed
black and blessed
…but never ever poor
again

Million Man March

a sea
an ocean
a flood of tears
and hugs
daps and slaps
nappy male love
one million caps
and crowns and
burnt brass faces
whoever said it was less
didn't count noses
or wet eyes
didn't hear the black thunder
echo
or feel the wave of trust
that almost launched
the Egyptian monument
pretending to belong
to washington
it's a new day black man
and an early Kwanzaa
for mothers and babies
who search
the stars at night
wishing for their sugar
looking for their daddies

one million men
no niggers
one million men
one soul
for real columbuses
re-discovering themselves
finally being woman enough to
give birth
to a new idea
new attitudes
a new direction
a new day

if only one
sober
solemn
sincere
son, brother, cousin, uncle
father, granddaddy, or husband
had shown up
it still would have been
one magnificent
holy day
…but it was
much more than that
a million times
more

The Harvest

(for my sigmas & zetas, deltas, omegas,
alphas, AKAs, gamma rhos, iotas & nupes)

we were planted deep
by one-with-God
agriculturalists
who looked to the heavens
for truth
before any such thing
as an almanac

we are the seeds
of osiris and isis
we know what the harvest
will bring

we never claim to be greek
for we know that the fraternal order
that was the model
for our predominantly black greek letter institutions
was itself
a poor imitation
of an african mystery school system
that turned out ancient scholars, priests, rulers
and public servants

having survived the horrific
middle passage
we planted ourselves in the soil
of this new world
harvesting the fruit by moonlight
saving the seeds
and passing them from
generation
to generation
seeds that produced
the harlem renaissance
anti-lynching campaigns
and civil rights movements
bearing fruit as ripe as
underground railroad conductors
buffalo soldiers
and black panthers

in full bloom
we have access
to a spirit that manifests itself
in what we discover as purpose
in our lives
planting our seeds
and using these greek letters
as tools

we do the work
that must be done
for we know
what the harvest will bring
and we honor
the wisdom and the courage
of our founders
by proactively selecting our battles
and living the african axiom:
'when spider webs unite
they can tie up a lion'

Dogon

what if we
finally remembered
how the dogon in us
sat crosslegged
on a rock
in the rain
closed our eyes
and traveled around the moon
and past the sun
how we
scooped up a handful
of earth
and charted the solar system
as it sifted through
our fingers
generations
of stars
at a time
forming symmetrical
red
clay
pyramids

twin   sand
breast   castles

n
our
heads

what if
we finally realized
the infinite power
of our collective wisdom
married to action
and simply
walked out onto space
passing through
all the barriers
that we let
hold us back
held hands
and thought
this is our earth
let us save it
for the children

Healer

church mother
yoruba high priestess
nandi
to the zulu
pentecostal scripture quotin'
holy water sprinklin'
talkin' in tongues
wearin' white
you studied nursing
to learn to disguise
your own ancient ways
your knowing hands
have prepared birth canals
tied umbilical cords
closed eyelids

you see the storm
before the crickets
your skin crawls
when evil lurks

you closed your fertile gates
long ago
to keep a more vigilant watch
over them that came

over them that were sent
to your shade tree
your front porch
your holy place

I saw you step inside
the weak
inside
the innocent
touch their pain
and shout it out

I saw you
anointed with olive oil
full of the holy spirit
reach down deep
and rebuild backbones
close holes in hearts
rescue lost smiles
and souls

when you said 'go'
I went
when you said
'do the right thing'
I gave the child my name
no questions asked

now you say
read ecclesiastes and weigh
my own struggles

study king solomon
and know real wisdom
you said
'this is just the beginning'
so I'm making room in my hope chest
and saving energy
believing
in your knowing
and praying ways

Fireproof

the heart
of the bible belt
is steepled
the souls of church folk
have pews
the home of gospel music
has been forever altered
because only a devil
could set fire
to a church

but church people
are like fire ants
as soon as the smoke clears
they'll be stirring up cement
testing new extinguishers
installing a smoke alarm
in the pulpit

before you can say
revelations
chapter twenty
verses seven through ten
they will stop moaning and wailing
and sift through the ashes

tip over charred and smoky stained glass
looking for the mourners' bench
and come Sunday
twice as many worshippers
will pray on it
from a cross
the street
under a tree
counting pennies
and their blessings
starting a new building fund
'til the roof is raised
and the foundation poured
again
thanking the Lord
for a new day
and their right minds
regretful for needing
such a powerful message
to continue believing
that God is good and wise and merciful
offering up prayers
for them that done the deed
asking the Lord
to touch their dark hearts
smother out all that evil
guide them
on a straighter narrower path

forever
forgiving

church people
are fireproof
and Faith
won't just go up
in smoke

Amazin' Grace

Amazing grace! how sweet the sound
That saved a wretch like me!
I once was lost, but now am found
Was blind, but now I see…

It isn't negro
but it is spiritual
it do speak to the power
of redemption
to power period
converting lost
to found
creating sight
where there was none
but what sound could be
so powerfully sweet
sweet enough
to turn a wretched
slave-ship captain
into england's most outspoken
abolitionist and songwriter

was it the splash of bodies
dragged kicking and screaming

jettisoned off decks
to the outstretched arms
of ocean coral
was it the crack of the whip
or the popping sound bloody flesh makes
when a sizzling branding iron
breaks the skin

the sound of fear and confusion
below deck
muffled by the sound of rape up above

the sound of 609 beating hearts
sardined into a space for 300

amazing is to be lost and blind
and still the captain
a willing participant
in crimes against humanity

but what was that sound
that liberating release
granting pardons
for penitence undone?
what does forgiveness sound like?

Thro' many dangers, toils and snares
I have already come…

now every time you hear amazing grace
listen for john newton's apology
his silent sobs seeking salvation
listen and hear
what healing sounds like

'Tis grace hath brought me safe thus far,
And grace will lead me home

A Wake

i thought you said
this was the Lord's house
i don't feel nothing in here
all these southern baptists
and no outburst
something's wrong
no real tears
just quiet respectful
organized sobbing
we don't need this priest
we need a church
with ministers
and a congregation
to moan and wail
to open up heaven's door so wide
that everyone knows
a chariot is coming
to take this black woman home
make some noise
damn it
stop that nice passive
latin chanting
ain't this a funeral
ain't that somebody's mother
laying there

find us one of those
aretha mahalia shirley caesar jackson
voices
to reach deep inside
and rip out
all of this sorrow
somebody scream
PLEASE
somebody get up
and fight the devil
for this soul
put some old black fingers
on that organ
and let them
make it
swing so low
that we fall out in the aisle
screaming
take me too je ... sus

she wasn't all good
but she was all ours
and we don't just give each other up
all nice and polite like
it ain't our way
it ain't never been
not this family

and if this is
the Lord's house
well He must still be asleep
because there's too many
nappy heads in here
for this to still be
a quiet catholic church

can i get an amen?

Red-Handed

even then
when I was knee high
to monochromatic parents
these hands were too big and loud
for small quiet me
they jutted out
from my mamma's skirt
demanding attention
pretending to be my eyes
trying to be my smile
they were solar powered
with curiosity
they could smell
and taste
and hear
they were my antennae
my personal digital
communications system
miniature satellite dishes

they swallowed books
whole
wrestled with pencils and crayons

danced in the air like kites
with answers
before teachers could finish the questions

they set fire
to my sister's hair
were deathly afraid
of soap and water
they recreated
science lab experiments
at home on the kitchen table
collected fossils, comics, moon rocks
junebugs and mexican jumping beans
they pointed out
shooting stars
and constellations
removed my glasses
after I fell asleep reading
and prayed for me at night

they grabbed those diplomas
and a map
and set off to see the world
fell in love
with the caribbean

reached out and touched
niagara falls and
never forgot the way back home
to danville

these hands aspire to be as
strong and comforting
as granddaddy's
when we grow up

they have always been
too big and loud
and now they've taken to
writing poems
and twisting my arm
to read them
aloud

Poetry Moments

here i stand
biting my tongue
and cheek
thanking these itinerant gypsies
for checking my homophobia
arresting my sexism
challenging
my ethnocentricity
long enough
to exchange prayers
to be the black pepper
in this fool stew
this all natural callaloo
of home grown
pearls and peanuts

taking off my war paint
postponing
the battle of little big horn
to ride bareback
in this kentucky derby
of words
letting my guard down
just enough
to sift through
the camouflage

and experience the pain
that brought today's new works
back up like vomit
and tossed into our
naked circle
like live
heart grenades

inspired by these
new zoras and langstons
who have discovered
that i am
the kind of poet
who likes to cuddle
after penning a piece

i lie here
exhausted
seduced by this
either or–gy
begging for cigarettes
and waiting for the moon
to dry
yet another sweat stained
silk page

Diamond Seed

Sweet brown girl
you lie belly up
your scar
dancing 'round your navel
like a Mississippi tributary
snaking its way
south
to the gulf
waiting to rock me
to that final
sleep

When I complete
my circle
before I am
buried beneath bluegrass
I will return
to you
deep and still
draped in silk
committed as kudzu
and evergreen
finally at rest
entombed in your warmth

your breath
your arms
pharaoh
of your earthen pyramid
to lie
to rest
to be
one more coal
in a quiet
Kentucky mountain

In Hell Exhale

if you listen to a woman breathe
she'll tell you exactly
what she's looking for
or if she's looking
at all
what she wants
what she needs
right there
in that light year
between breaths
she will draw you a picture
a picture so real
you can become a part
of the very thing she desires
or choose to steal away
before the dawn
if you stay
train up your ears
because what she wants
needs or desires
is subject to change
in a heartbeat

but always remember
if you commit
be sure
and hold your ground
but never
ever
hold
your breath
because be sure
she's also listening
to you

Mermaid
(for Raina)

you dolphin your wet skin
against mine
teaching me to swim
inviting me to dive
with you
to unknown depths
deep beneath
the comforters and quilts
at the bottom of the bed
you rock
your hips
and waves
and watch as your ocean
pulls me under
like a sea toy
anchored
in piles
of discarded cottons
and silks

afloat
like driftwood
trapped in seaweed sheets
I surrender

to currents
that wash me ashore
gasping for breath
where I lie and wait
for the tide
to carry me
back out
again

Stop Looking and Listen

*The problem of the 20th century is the problem
of the color line.* – W. E. B. Du Bois

I see you there
want to say
I know you
want more
for you to know yourself
have watched you
in my classrooms
in my bedroom
clinging to my eyeteeth
waving your blackness
like a signal flare
flexing your nostrils
rolling your neck hard
lest some new nigga
mistake you
for the enemy
i remember the day
you stopped apologizing
for being
'high yella'
answering to 'redbone'
accepting compliments
for your 'good' hair

and made that speech
about how ain't none of us
as pure
as we claim to be
acknowledging
your europe
claiming your cherokee
embracing your africa
all of them
all at once
and daring us to do
the same
saying that erasing
even one ancestor
negates our very existence
you scream at the world
every time
the issue of color
tips the scales
of justice
then you scream at me
and i whisper back
to you
reminding that
i've never asked you
to change your hair
just your mind

because our children
must always
love themselves
and honoring
the beautiful ugly
blood
that courses through
their veins
will make them
as strong
as you
are
now

My Boy D'
(for Taajwar Dvan Howard)

Dvan
why you put your gum
on the door?
cause, cause alla sweet gone out
Oh
mamma, i mean daddy
guess what
What D?
when, when
when, i take a bath
my hands and feet
turn old
Really?
yeah, and and guess what else
What D?
my, my mamma an an
my otha daddy
they taked me to the zoo
an da aminals
they wuz lookin at me
Did they try'n keep you?
NO, DAD!
they just keeped lookin
at me

Did you like the zoo?
yeah, yeah i did
i liked it
... dad
What D?
can i, can i go home wif you?
Sure lil' man
can, can my mamma come too?
Uhhhh ... you got any more
of that gum?

Nikki
(for Tamirra Nicole Walker)

your new woman ways
are playing
hide 'n seek
with what used to be
daddy's lil' gurl
i be stepping back
stretching out both arms
not to let you go
just to give you more room
to grow
while i stand behind you
in the mirror
watching you try on
your mamma's
hips

Ed Works
(for Ed Hamilton)

caramel colored
ankh-utech
kneading life into earth
like the first One
who scooped up
a lump of clay
and xeroxed
his/her own image

the lips
on your hands
the eyes on your
fingertips
transport ancestors
back from the dead
in forms so real
they breathe life
into us

Glory-us
sigh-entist
more cassius than clay
translating spirit
rescuing history

sculpting our lives
into monumental
bronze
photographs
watching you work
is like
watching God
play
leaving no doubt
you both used
the same model
me/us

thank you
for your vision
you vessel
you caramel colored
ankh-utech
you knead our back
and we will always
need yours

Jíbaros
(for Ricardo Nazario Colón)

Tú eres mi hermano
mi jíbaro
the hypotenuse
of the golden triangle
that graphed itself
from spanish docks
to african shores
to the americas
via another cristóbal theft
puerto rico
the rich port

Tú eres mi hermano
richie
mami Francisca's
pasteles y coquito
sit forever
on my tongue
apologizing for my
k-mart spanish
i will be belly warm
and bacardi full
forever

Like romulus and remus
separated at birth
spirited away from our regal domain
raised by los jíbaros de caña
earthpeople
taino y caribe
blackfoot &
ashanti
worshippers del sol
we now return to claim
our dual heritage

Disguised
as international scribes
priests & thieves
dropping culture
littering the earth
with crescents
and murals
adventuring to atlantic oceans
caribbean seas
appalachian mountains
knowing the tombstones
will show us the way
home
el camino al hogar
viajando a las sepulturas
de los magnos
hombres negros

black rock gardens
brushing off snow
dripping juice
inhaling a ceremonial
cigar
bendíseme aire
que respiramos
blessing the very air
we breathe

Tú eres mi hermano
ricardo
almas azules y blancas
de Faith y Francisca
mamas' boys
criados de pecho
breast babies
umbilically linked
forever homogenized
para que todo el mundo sepa
to see, to know

Somos familia
frater colón
our seeds
will inherit the earth

Sara Yevo

forcing the words
through her teeth
stabbing the air
with a frown
she declared
'I do not like that word!
I do not like anything that separates
people
by region
or culture or class'

I could only listen
could only focus on
the sharp images
in her mental photo album

pointing to the scars in the air
she leaked out
'I am a refugee
I came to this country
three years ago
from Bosnia'
she left everything she knew
because the earth and the sky
divorced
and there was no middle
to stand in

'why would I embrace division?
how could i wrap my arms
around a carcinogen
when division
kills?'

I wanted to tell her
that the word Affrilachia
was not intended to take lives
was not intended to destroy families
or divide communities
that it existed to make visible
to create a sense of place
that had not existed
for us
for any unwealthy common
people of color
now claiming the dirt
they were born in

I instead said nothing
thinking she would not understand
only recently divided
unfamiliar with our own
un civil war
she could not know
while scanning the room
and seeing only fat happy
americans

tucked safely away in the mountains
of west virginia
no hillbillies, no niggers
not even poverty
married to the coal
beneath our nails
just under our skin

she immigrated into our classroom
seeking asylum
carrying only her own wounds
and none of our
ever present racial baggage
or our painful history
of abduction, slavery
rape, lynchings, castrations
our own north american
apartheid-flavored democracy

she was already free
more free
than we could ever be
as we could never see ourselves
truly indivisible
because our history
enslaves us
and only amnesia could
overthrow who we've become
and finally set us free

Indiana

was scared at first
of indiana
tales of ku kluxers
and smiling white racists
Marion's 60-year young lynching

hadn't seen anything like
all this grandfather straight corn
since i stood
on the capitol steps
and smiled out at the
million
heads and shoulders
planted
ear to ear
blanketing everything
between
democracy's shadow
and abraham lincoln's
feats
nothing like those
arms outstretched
believing in the sun
fields of dreams
since those renewed nappy stalks
held hands and prayed

on washington's lawn
a bumper crop of atonement
weeding themselves
unwilling to let
the seedlings
rot in the field
or be used
to soak up
stomach acid
in the hungry belly
of a nation feeding on itself
yet
starving for change

was scared at first
of indiana
and its mysterious
corn silk oceans
but now i see
my grandfather
there
and a million newborn men
in the shadows
of the green horizon
teaching me
to stand up straight
and how to
corn row
my fears

Affrilachia
(for gurney & anne)

thoroughbred racing
and hee haw
are burdensome images
for kentucky sons
venturing beyond the mason–dixon

anywhere in appalachia
is about as far
as you could get
from our house
in the projects
yet
a mutual appreciation
for fresh greens
and cornbread
an almost heroic notion
of family
and porches
makes us kinfolk
somehow
but having never ridden
bareback
or sidesaddle

and being inexperienced
at cutting
hanging
or chewing tobacco
yet still feeling
complete and proud to say
that some of the bluegrass
is black
enough to know
that being 'colored' and all
is generally lost
somewhere between
the dukes of hazzard
and the beverly hillbillies
but
if you think
makin' 'shine from corn
is as hard as kentucky coal
imagine being
an Affrilachian
poet

Breakfast in Hazard

Thick as grits
or biscuit gravy
fog gathers in the night
like a quilt
wrapping itself 'round
everything
making an island
of this high ridge turned
holiday inn
carved straight out of
bedrock

Drawn tight against
the fence
a quiet cover
of handspun
cotton and wool
spiders
out of the coffee
and blankets the sky
on mountain
mornings

Kentucke
(for James Still)

Kentucke
once bloody ground
hunting Eden
for native tongues
apologetically eliminating buffalo
for sustenance
not sport or profit
or pleasure

un common wealth
repopulated
with immigrants
and freedmen
who discovered black lung
was as indiscriminate
as calluses
& hunger

you remain north & south
interstate highways
your crucifix
blessing yourself with
64 and I-75

you have derbied
and dribbled yourself
a place in a world
that will not let you forget
you
co-Rupped basketball
your cash crop causes cancer
& the run for the roses
is only two minutes long

kin tucky
beautiful ugly
cousin
i too am of these hills
my folks
have corn rowed
tobacco
laid track
strip mined
worshipped & whiskied
from Harlan to Maysville
old Dunbar to Central

our whitney youngs
and mae street kidds
cut their teeth
on bourbon balls

and though
conspicuously absent
from millionaires row
we have isaac murphied
our way
down the back stretch
cassius clayed
our names in cement
we are the amen
in church hill downs
the mint
in the julep
we put the heat
in the hotbrown
and
gave it color
indeed
some of the bluegrass
is black

Clifton II

If I thought
it made a difference
I'd round up everybody I know
bring them to this place
this Clifton
let them see
what used to be
ours.
If I thought it mattered
I'd bring my son and daughter
my nieces and nephews
to the old schoolhouse
and draw detailed maps
in the air
that highlighted
the thirty-three beautiful acres
bordered by the long slow curve
of the dix river.
If I thought they'd listen
I'd produce a powerpoint presentation
featuring all the faded yellow photographs
in aunt willie's archives.
I'd point to clean white dresses
leather boots and knickers

and the serious look on granddaddy's
ten-year-old face
and how much we all
favored each other
even then
even under a hat.
I'd pass around
a restored print
of their great great grandmother
margaret
who passed when mamma e
was just six months old
hoping they recognized
the high cheekbones
and regal disposition
that survived five generations
of mothers and daughters
and deaths
boldly suggesting that
their own beauty wasn't accidental
that it was actually a precious family heirloom.
Projecting an IMAX-sized photo
of mamma e's graduating class
on the wall
I'd draw attention
to the proud and focused faces
standing and kneeling
in two-feet-high weeds

wearing dark caps and gowns
like gold crowns and kente
clutching diplomas
like freedom passes
holding on to each other
with their eyes.
If I thought it was worth the effort
I would try not to be too anxious
or too teary eyed
while I hoped at least one of them
would memorize these things
and pass it on
until it mattered.

ABOUT THE AUTHOR

Frank X Walker is a native of
Danville, Kentucky. His poetry has appeared
in numerous journals and anthologies.
Affrilachia is his first book.